Wandering Woman: New Mexico

The Ultimate Road Trip: One Woman's Journey Across the United States by Car

Julie Bettendorf

Contents

Introduction

"Not all who wander are lost."

Are you sure? I thought to myself, as I tried not to panic. I was a long way from anything familiar, but that was how it should be. I had driven thousands of miles on dusty, pothole-filled roads. It's often on the worst roads that you can discover something truly amazing.

My dusty CRV was parked beside me, containing one restless dog and a variety of snack bags, all empty by now. There were no buildings in sight, no cars or people or movement at all. Only the constant humming of the insects as they buzzed around my head.

I turned to my left – another straight road that trailed off into the distance. I glanced over to the right, then behind me – two more barely discernible roads stretched out into the abyss. I was in a four-way intersection with no signs, no sense of direction, and no sign of life for several miles. No cell service either. *Damn*, I thought. *I'm lost.*

How did I get here? I couldn't help but feel like this little intersection was a cruel metaphor for life. I began to daydream, imagining each road might transport me back to a different time, a different role in my life, and a different me.

If I took the road from whence I came, it could lead me all the way back to Oregon, back to my cheating third husband, back to a life of loneliness and solitude. There is no greater loneliness than being married to someone who isn't actually present in your life.

If I took the road to my left, perhaps it could take me back to my career as a dental hygienist, a job I hated deep down in my soul. There is something so disengaging about cleaning teeth for a living. It's a disgusting, smelly way to get a paycheck. It pays well, which is great, but the best part is the huge gob of friends I enjoy to this day.

Or maybe the road to my right, *yes – maybe that's the path*, I imagined. Maybe it could take me back to my real treasure, my kids. Back to their smiling, innocent faces as toddlers, as they danced around the Christmas tree and their father and I were still married. Back when they still needed me for every little thing.

But, that was just it. I didn't feel needed anymore. My kids weren't toddlers anymore – they were both full-grown adults, and far too busy for me. My dental buddies were still working, but I wasn't. Dental hygiene had robbed me of the cartilage in my fingers, giving me severe, disabling arthritis. And, I wouldn't be returning to any more husbands either, because three marriages were quite enough for me.

All three of these paths, all three of these roles – the wife, the mother, and the dental hygienist – had seemingly been stripped from me within a year. I was lost and looking to find myself again.

The funny thing about this phrase, "not all who wander are lost" – is that, in my experience, wandering and being lost walk hand-in-hand with one another, and the expression can be flipped. In my experience, not all who are lost are wandering, and that is a real disservice to the beauty and clarity that the world has to offer.

When one becomes lost, wandering is the only option to guide oneself back to a path. After all, one could not come upon any dirt path at all without wandering.

I began wandering at an early age, both with my mind and with my feet. At eight years old, I was reading a book about archaeology and dreaming of one day seeing Egypt. I didn't follow a traditional path in high school either, going heavily into foreign languages, in hopes of one day using them.

At twenty-five years old, I divorced my first husband (the dental student who talked me into becoming a dental hygienist so I could work for him) and decided to give traveling a real shot. I took off for the Andes and Macchu Picchu, climbing up ancient Inca stone steps to reach the magnificent ruins.

Anyone who has been to Macchu Picchu will tell you there is something ethereal and deeply spiritual about the place. The ruins stretch out across the emerald green mountains, way up in the middle of the sky. Macchu Picchu gave me my first experience of feeling history. This trip inspired me to come back and complete a degree in archaeology, and I've been wandering ever since.

More travel followed including a backpack trip around Europe for three months, by myself, and trips to Britain, Italy, and Greece. I visited the burial places of Crusaders, mummies, and ancient kings. I happened upon the castle of my namesake in Bettendorf, Luxembourg, and wandered my way through European history.

My favorite excursion by far was finally seeing Egypt with my daughter in 2012. Just like my childhood dream envisioned, I rode a camel beneath the pyramids of Giza, with my head wrapped in some man's sweaty turban. It was perfect.

Traveling has always been my own personal antidote to pain. I went to Mexico after my first and second divorces, Canada after my third, and Italy after my dad died. Call it avoidance if you want, but I call it an accelerated form of healing in the purest sense of the word. I believe travel can heal your soul.

Wandering has always worked its wonders on me – made me feel renewed, rejoiceful, grateful, and purposeful. It's been my medicine.

So, as I stood in that intersection, I once again wondered how wandering had led me so astray this time. ***What the hell am I supposed to do now?*** It was then that I realized that one last path had not been considered yet – the path which stretched straight out in front of me. ***Which role does this represent?*** I pondered.

The answer smacked me in the face.

That last dirt road – the only path that could take me where I wanted to go, the only path that ever truly healed me or showed me the way – was the path of the traveler. The wife, the mother, and the hygienist roles – though valued in their time – were sitting in the bleachers now. It was time to welcome and enable my boldest, bravest, and perhaps most pivotal role yet:

The role of the Wandering Woman.

Welcome to Wandering Woman

This book is for you – the grieving empty nester mom, the begrudged housewife, the woman in need of a drastic change in her life. Really, this book is for anyone with a passion for traveling. If you feel lost with no sense of direction or purpose in life, that's a bonus – this book will be even more appealing to you. And lastly, if you're a man reading this book, congratulations for holding a book with the word woman in the title. You're contributing to gender equality, and that's pretty neat.

I decided to combine three of my dearest loves – travel, history, and archaeology – and put them into a book because I believe wandering has the power to change your life. I have been to many areas of the world and had too many outstanding experiences to list. However, by the time both my children had

Me

moved out in 2017, I had never seen my own country – America. It was the perfect time to explore a new country (my own) and discover a new me at the same time.

So, I packed up my Honda CRV, along with some gear and my 14-year-old furry friend, Sadie. ***Wandering Woman*** is the chronicle of my journey across eleven states, discovering the joy of getting lost and finding myself along the way.

Why America?

A *merica, the beautiful?* I sure think so, but I didn't realize just
how beautiful our country is until I embarked on traveling
across eleven western states in a year.

The United States offers everything for the discerning palate.
From spectacular beaches, austere mountains, to rolling plains,
our country has it all. It's difficult to comprehend just how large
and impressive our scenery is, until you experience it first-hand,
with the ultimate road trip.

I also realized just how much of
our history is missing from U.S.
history I was taught as a kid. The
history of our country didn't begin with the pilgrims landing on
Plymouth Rock in the 1600s. Our
history is far more ancient, with
rock art and archaeological sites
dating back over 12,000 years.

We also owe a tremendous debt to early pioneers who tamed
our land. The Mormons and other groups ventured into the great
unknown with their families and their worldly possessions. Some

of them pulled cumbersome handcarts across the country to settle in inhospitable, dangerous locations.

The goal of Wandering Woman is to bring history back to life and make it interesting again. I am presenting some famous sites, and many little-known ones. You will take the road-less-traveled with me, while we explore ghost towns, rock art sites, archaeological sites, and museums, to discover the colorful tapestry that is our country.

I present some history, including dates, but my goal is to present more of the real-life stories of history, including ghost stories, profiles in history, voices from the past, and moments in time, to give you, the reader, a deeper understanding of the context of history.

This is by no means an exhaustive list of places to visit. In fact, I encourage you to discover America for yourself, as I did, by making a trek across the land by car. You can explore as the early explorers did, just a little more comfortably, with a lot less hardship.

I hope you enjoy this book and take a little time out to discover our beautiful country, and maybe even discover yourself in the process.

Safe Travels,

Julie Bettendorf

Welcome to New Mexico

Land of Enchantment

New Mexico is called the "Land of Enchantment" for good reason. There is something very spiritual about the state, with its centuries-old Spanish missions and vast stretches of desolate landscape, peppered with small villages of a few people. As I write this, I am looking out at Storrie Lake, watching the sun set. I highly recommend Storrie Lake Campground just outside of Las Vegas, New Mexico, and the City of Rocks Campground to introduce yourself to the beauty of New Mexico.

5 things to love about New Mexico:

Billy the Kid history of sites like Lincoln and Fort Sumner

Charming old town Albuquerque and old town Santa Fe

The history written-in-stone in places like El Morro

Old Spanish missions like Jemez, Quarai, Abo, and Gran Quivira

The random cattle drives in the middle of the road

Top Stuff to See in New Mexico

Top Archaeological Sites:

- Gila Cliff Dwellings

- Bandelier National Monument

Top Historical Sites:

- El Morro National Monument

- Jemez Historic Site

Top Museums:

- Art and History Museum in Albuquerque

- Billy the Kid Museum in Fort Sumner

Top Natural Wonders:

- Carlsbad Caverns

- Blackwater Draw

When driving through New Mexico, be on the lookout for:

J avelinas or wild pigs, deer, and livestock, often in the middle of the road

Early New Mexico

Early Visitors to Blackwater Draw

Early Lincoln, New Mexico

Early Visitors to Pecos

Dreams of New Mexico

"I think New Mexico was the greatest experience from the outside world that I have ever had."— **D. H. Lawrence**

"Until I came to New Mexico, I never realized how much beauty water adds to a river."— **Mark Twain**

"I think spiritual perception comes from natural and healthy relationship to the land and I've had that. I get an easy, automatic sense of myself in nature, a wholeness and I feel nowhere else. I think people should live where praying is most immediate. That's why I live in New Mexico. The physical terrain, the feeling, the environment and culture improve my life just by waking up ther e."— **Val Kilmer**

Northwestern New Mexico

El Morro National Monument

Chaco Culture National Historic Park

The road into ***Chaco Culture National Historic Park*** is about 20 miles of washboard roughness that will jiggle your teeth as you drive. It's a dusty drive, and the environment looks forbidding. It's not a spot you would think a complex society would decide to build. But not only did they build, the people created a unique world, known as the Chaco culture.

Chaco Canyon structures were built in stages between 800 AD through 1100 AD with most active building begun in 1050 AD. The Chaco culture had a system of outlying communities with kivas, a great house, and a complex system of over 400 miles of road.

The roads were 30 feet across and built to go up and over obstacles. Noble, NPS

Buildings were often oriented to solar, lunar, and cardinal directions. The great houses had lines of sight to each other, to help with communication.

One of the larger structures, **_Pueblo Bonito_**, had 4 stories and at least 600 rooms. During excavations at Pueblo Bonito, one of the rooms contained the remains of 14 people, buried with over 50,000 pieces of turquoise, including a necklace of 2000 turquoise beads,  thousands of shell ornaments, and a basket covered with a turquoise mosaic.

The structures were built with an intricate veneer masonry made up of a core of rubble or mud and wood supports, with veneers of small and large precisely cut stones laid over the core.

They would often plaster over and paint many of the beautifully laid out walls. As a result, Chaco has some spectacular pictographs and petroglyphs. The Chaco culture fell apart around 1140AD, coinciding with a severe drought.

How to get to Chaco Culture National Historic Park:

Chaco Culture National Historic Park is in a remote location, about 55 miles from the town of Bloomfield, in northwestern New Mexico.

A word about what happened:

What happened to these ancient cultures which caused them to abandon their monumental buildings:

- The Mimbres culture disappeared around 1130 AD

- Chaco Canyon, North Black Mesa, and Ancestral Puebloan all disappeared middle to late 1100's

- Mesa Verde and Kayenta cultures disappeared around 1300 AD

- Mogollon culture disappeared around 1400 AD

- Hohokam disappeared late into the 1400's

It was probably a combination of factors that caused the residents to abandon their homes. One of the main causes was a major multi-year drought beginning around 1130 AD. Cultures were impacted differently by this, depending on whether they lived in an area with more or less rainfall. Those that lived at higher elevations with more rainfall tended to cope with the drought better.

Cultures with larger populations like Chaco Canyon, exhausted their food supply more quickly, resulting in conflict over food, land, and other resources. There is some evidence of cannibalism, because human muscle protein has been found in the dried fecal material of ancient humans. Major conflict was inevitable, and it is widely believed that ancient survivors were absorbed into other cultures like the Zuni. Diamond

El Morro National Monument

El Morro National Monument is a fantastic place; in fact, it's one of my favorite sights to see. El Morro means "the headland" or "the bluff" and it is a large sandstone outcropping in the middle of a golden prairie. There are over 2000 inscriptions and petroglyphs carved into the rock. The ruins of a 700 year old pueblo, named *Atsinna*, lie at the top of the bluff. The Pueblo was inhabited from 1275 AD to 1350 AD and reached a population of around 1500 people. Noble, NPS

There is a naturally-formed pool at El Morro which is fed by rainwater. The pool can reach 12 feet deep and hold 200,000 gallons of water. This natural pool made El Morro a popular stopping place across the centuries.

The inscriptions begin with petroglyphs which date back to 1100 AD. It is believed these were made using hammer stones.

The writings of Spanish con-quistadors date from 1539 to 1774. The first governor of New Mexico, Don Juan de Onate, left a message in 1605, 15 years be-fore the Pilgrims landed on Ply-mouth Rock. The Spanish used daggers or horseshoe nails to make their marks.[Slater]

The early pioneers left their marks at El Morro too, from the years 1846 to 1906, when feder-al law was established to prohib-it future carving. Early pioneers used knives, nails, or chisels to leave their inscriptions.

How to get to El Morro National Monument:

El Morro National Monument is located near the town of Ramah, off Hwy. 53, in Western New Mexico.

These are just a few of the many inscriptions at El Morro:

"There passed this way the Adelantado Don Juan de Onate, from the discovering of the South Sea, on the 16th of April, 1605" **An-**

tonio de Espejo, March 11, 1583, Don Juan de Onate, April 16, 1605

"passed by here in the year of 1636" **Sergeant Major Juan de Arechuleta and Adjutant Diego Martin Barba.** Arechuleta came with Onate in 1598 to colonize New Mexico. Arechuleta and Barba were beheaded in the plaza in Santa Fe in 1643 for their parts in a plot to assassinate the colonial governor.

"Here was the General Don diego de Vargas, who conquered for our Holy faith, and for the Royal Crown, all the New Mexico at his expense, year of 1692" **Don Diego de Vargas 1692**

Among the early pioneer inscriptions is that of America Baley, who signed in 1858. Her party of 60 was attacked by 800 Mojave Indians. Nine pioneers were killed and 17 injured. 87 Mojave died. America Baley survived and made it to California.

Beale and Breckinridge, signed in 1857. P. (Peachy) Breckenridge was the person in charge of the 25 camels brought to New Mexico in 1857. He later returned to Virginia and fought in the Civil War. Breckenridge was killed in a battle at Kennon's Landing in 1863.

E. Penn Long of the US Army, signed his name at El Morro, probably during his second visit in 1859. From 1857-1859 he was part of a group. NPS

Voices from the past:

"...here were indeed inscriptions of interest, if not of value, one of them dating as far back as 1606, all of them very ancient, and several of them very deeply as well as beautifully engraven..." **report**

of Lieutenant Simpson, Corps of Topographical Engineers, September 17, 1849.

When you visit El Morro today, you can see the inscription left behind by Simpson and his men: *Lt. J.H. Simpson, U.S.A. and R.H. Kern, artist, visited and copied these inscriptions, September 17, 1849.*

Albuquerque

 lbuquerque is a great city, with a lot to offer, especially the ***Old Town***, where I had some delicious stuffed sopapillas at a wonderful outdoor café and art market. The outdoor venue is a great place to wander for a few hours.

The city was founded in 1706, as an important settlement on the Rio Grande, and part of the Camino Real.

I started my tour with the ***San Felipe De Neri Church***, established in 1793, during the Spanish Colonial period.

It's a beautiful church, both inside and out, and the grounds are spacious and inviting. Balfour

There is a must-see **_Art and History Museum_** in Albuquerque. When I visited, there was an outstanding exhibition of Treasures from Spain, including a door knocker collection, with pieces from the 1500s.

The exquisite pieces ranged from textiles, to illuminated books and pages, to pottery and ceramics.

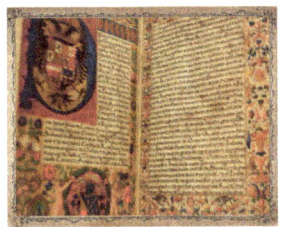

One of my favorite pieces was a Spanish Visigoth buckle from 500 AD, beautifully inlaid with garnets.

Another interesting piece is a 1470 Spanish brigandine, which was a leather tunic often used in place of armor. The unfortunate wearer of the brigandine was hit by a musket shot, which pierced the tunic.

There was also a vicious looking dog collar included in the collection. I doubt this dog was a pet.

One of the most amazing pieces in the collection is a world map, drawn by Giovanni Vespucci in 1527. The map is at least 8 feet long and it has marvelous little figures of animals, castles, ships, and people drawn on it. It's impossible to capture the beauty of the piece, but this small section gives you some idea.

Albuquerque has a little some-thing for everyone, including a **Rattlesnake Museum**, for those hard-to-please types.

How to get to Albuquerque historic sites:

San Felipe De Neri Church is located at 2005 N Plaza St NW.

The Art and History Museum is located at 2000 Mountain Rd NW.

The Rattlesnake Museum is located at 202 San Felipe St NW.

Coronado Historic Site

The fabulous **_Coronado Historic Site_** is a first contact site, similar in importance to Jamestown, Virginia, which was established in 1607, and Plymouth, Massachusetts which was established in 1620. The amazing fact is, this site is even earlier, dating to 1540.

When Coronado came to New Mexico in 1540, he found a pueblo called Kuaua, containing over 1200 rooms. Kuaua was at the crossroads of trade between the Pacific and Mexico.

The pueblo was built by the Tiwa, who lived in the pueblo from 1300 AD to 1600 AD. They ate corn, beans, and squash, raised herbs, raised turkeys and made blankets out of the feathers. Tiwa men wove cotton into garments.
Noble, NM Dept. of Cult. Affairs

Today, the remnants of the *pueblo* have been excavated and then backfilled to prevent damage. The structures visible are reconstructions to show what the pueblo looked like in 1540. In 1935, *murals* were discovered at the site. The murals turned out to be 17 layers of murals, with the earliest dating to 1500 AD. They

are now located in a special room, and there are absolutely no photographs allowed.

There is also an onsite *museum*, containing Tiwa artifacts and items dating from the contact with Coronado.

How to get to Coronado Historic Site:

Take exit 242 off Interstate 25, then take Hwy. 550 1.7 miles west to Kuaua Road.

Voices from the past:

"Tiguex is a province of twelve pueblos, on the banks of a large and mighty river. Some of the pueblos are on one bank, some on the other. It is a spacious valley two leagues wide. To the east there is a snow-covered sierra, very high and rough." **Pedro de Castaneda 1540**

"We visited a good many of these pueblos. They are all well built with straight, well-squared walls. Their towns have no defined streets. Their houses are three, five, six and even seven stories high, with many windows and terraces. The men spin and weave and the women cook, build houses, and keep them in good repair...they are quiet, peaceful people of good appearance and excellent physique, alert and intelligent." **Gaspar Perez de Villagra 1610.**

A word about the Coronado Expedition:

Coronado left Compostela in 1540, when he was 31 years old. He was searching for the 7 cities of Cibola and the golden treasure that awaited him there. The expedition consisted of 400 Spaniards, 1500 native American allies, 4 Franciscan friars, dozens of African slaves, and 6500 head of livestock including horses, cattle, sheep, and pigs.

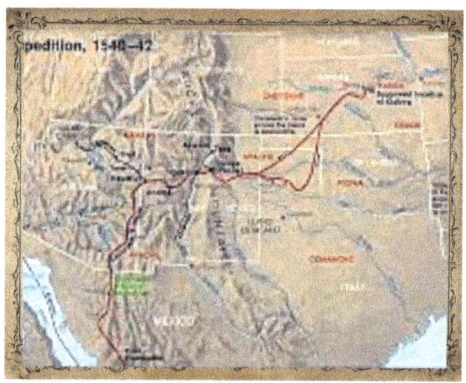

By the time they reached Kuaua, they were starving, so they took advantage of the Tiwa by lodging with them and eating their food. In 1541 the Tiwa rebelled, resulting in deaths of hundreds of Tiwas and the destruction of 2 villages. Coronado eventually reached

Kansas, the Grand Canyon, and Colorado in his quest for gold, before he turned back.

Profiles in history:

Juan Vázquez de Coronado was born in 1510. He was the illegitimate son of a Spanish nobleman and a Spanish woman of noble birth. Coronado was only 17 when he went to the Americas, first to Mexico, and then to Guatemala. He is most famous for the expedition he undertook in 1540, through what is now New Mexico, the Grand Canyon, Colorado, and Kansas, searching for the legendary 7 cities of Cibola. He married in 1548 and became Alcalde Mayor of San Salvador in 1549.

Coronado later became Alcalde Mayor of Honduras in 1556, and Nicaragua in 1561, before finally settling in Costa Rica in 1562. Coronado traveled to Spain, where King Phillip granted him the governorship of Costa Rica in 1565. Coronado was on his way back to Costa Rica when his ship was caught in a storm off of Southern Spain, and he was never heard from again.

Jemez Historic Site

Jemez Historic Site is a serene and beautiful place located high in the mountains. When I visited, the ground was covered in snow, and Jemez was sparkling and beautiful.

At Jemez, there are the ruins of the ancient village of Giusewa, home to the Hemesh, which the Spaniards turned into Jemez.

In 1540, Coronado came into the area and sent a group led by Captain Francisco de Barrionuevo who visited Giusewa. In 1598, Don Juan de Onate led settlers into the area. The first church was built there that same year.

The ruins standing today date from 1621, and are known as the San Jose de los Jemez Mission. The mission itself was designed by Fray Geronimo Zarate Salmeron and was only used for 20 years. It was abandoned in

1640. Noble, New Mexico Department of
Cultural Affairs

There were once beautiful frescoes painted on the walls, and pedestals are all that are left from saint statues that once lined the walls.

Today, as you walk the grounds, you can see the ruins of the *mission church*, the *Spanish administration offices*, *living quarters*, a *cemetery*, *courtyard*, and a secure *storeroom*, which was used to control the population's access to food and seed.

How to get to Jemez Historic Site:

Take exit 242 off I-25, then take Hwy. 550 west to San Ysidro, turn onto Route 4 and continue 18 miles.

Voices from the past:

"We gathered this tribe into two pueblos-namely San Jose which was still standing, with a breathtaking, sumptuous, and distinguished church and friary, and San Diego de la Congregacion...we gave them houses already built ,along with food and sustenance for several days and plowed fields for their seed plots...and although over half of this nation has died, your majesty may still count here on more than three thousand newly assembled taxpayers." **Fray Alonso de Benavides, 1630**

North Central
New Mexico

Pecos National Historic Park

Bandelier National Monument

The *Bandelier National Monument* is named for famous Southwest explorer Adolph Bandelier who visited in 1880. Bandelier National Monument is in a spectacular setting, surrounded by rugged hills.

The first people lived in the area 10,000 years ago, followed by the archaic people from 5500 BC to 600 AD. Noble, Western National Parks Association

Ancestral Puebloan people settled here, in dwellings formed from carved out volcanic ash layers. Tree ring dating dates the structures to 600 years ago.

The area reached a maximum population 0f 500 people by the late 1400s.

There are some mural fragments and faint petroglyphs at Bandelier, including a turkey.

How to get to Bandelier National Monument:

Bandelier National Monument is located near Los Alamos at 15 Entrance Rd.

A word about dendrochronology:

Dendrochronology is the study of tree rings, to find out the age of wood. It's a useful technique for archaeologists, climatologists, and other scientific disciplines. A core sample is taken from a piece of wood and compared against other samples in the same geographic location, which have known dates. When the tree rings match, the date of the wood can be determined.

Tree rings provide a record of catastrophic events too, including forest fires, droughts, earthquakes, and insect infestations. Typically, a year of growth is equal to one tree ring. During a period of wet climate, the tree ring will be wide, and during a dry climate, the tree ring will be narrower. Dendrochronology can help determine the age of wooden buildings, wood beams which were cut as posts for other building materials, and many other aspects of history and archaeology.

Profiles in history:

Adolph Bandelier was born in Bern, Switzerland, in 1840. He came to the United States at an early age, along with his family. They settled in Illinois and young Adolph began work in the family business. He soon became disenchanted with the work he was doing. He turned to studying native cultures of the Southwestern United States, Mexico. and South America. Adolph Bandelier traveled and explored extensively, authoring works on archaeology and ethnography. He died in 1914 in Seville, Spain.

Santa Fe

*S*anta Fe is delightful, and popular. The architecture alone makes it a must-see, but there is also a lot of history in the city. Franciscan friars came into New Mexico in 1598 and Santa Fe was founded in 1610. Life between the Spaniards living in Santa Fe and the native Pueblo Indians was anything but peaceful. In 1675, 4 pueblo Indians were executed for murdering Spaniards, and 40 other pueblo Indians were whipped for practicing sorcery. Just a few years later, the Pueblo Indian Revolt began.

I started my tour of Santa Fe with the ***Cathedral Basilica of St. Francis of Assisi***. The church was established in 1610, and a new church was built in 1629. This church was burnt down in the Pueblo Indian Revolt in 1680.

Cathedral Basilica of St. Francis of Assisi

Another new church was built in 1714. This church was rebuilt and enlarged in the early 1800s. The current cathedral was dedicated in 1886.

As you walk around the Cathedral, you will see the Conquis-
tadora statue. It was created in
Spain in the 1400s and brought to
Santa Fe in 1625. The statue of St.
Francis on the altar screen dates
from the 1700s.

There is also a reliquary in the
Cathedral which is said to con-
tain a piece of the Holy Cross,
a piece of the veil of the Virgin
Mary, a bone from St. Francis of
Assisi, and the skull cap of Pope
John Paul II.

Another beautiful historical Santa Fe church is the **San Miguel
Mission and Church.** The earliest church was built by Tlax-
calan Indians who came with
Don Juan Onate in 1598. A second church was built in 1610.
There were many additional re-

constructions made over several centuries. San Miguel Chapel

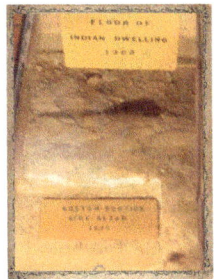

In 1955, a Spanish Colonial Art Expert headed up the final reconstruction and uncovered the original floor and sanctuary steps which you can see through clear windows beyond the communion railing. Human remains were also found buried under the church floor.

Today, as you walk around the San Miguel church, you will see several items of historical interest, beginning with the altar screen which reads: *"This altar was erected through the piety of Don Jose Antonio Ortis in the year 1798".*

In the center is a statue of San Miguel (St. Michael) carved in 1700. This statue was brought by the Franciscan friars to Santa Fe. Other figures date from the early to mid 1700s.

One of the wooden support-
ing beams reads *"El Marques
of Penuela had this construction erected by his royal ensign
Agustin Flores Vergada in the
year 1710"*.

The world famous **Loretto
Chapel** is also in Santa Fe. The
beautiful chapel was built in 1873
and is the first Gothic building
west of the Mississippi. It was
styled after the Sainte Chapelle
Cathedral in Paris.

It's famous for its staircase,
which has no visible means of
support.

No trip to Santa Fe is complete without a visit to the *New Mexico History Museum*. It has many interesting pieces including a wonderful tortoiseshell ladies headpiece.

The museum has a little something for everyone, including Civil War artifacts, and a magnificent 1926 painting of a parade by Gustave Baumann.

There are also several examples of Spanish weapons and armor from various Spanish explorations, including the search for the Seven Cities of Cibola.

The most macabre piece in the museum is the death mask of Mexican revolutionary Pancho Villa, who was assassinated in Mexico in 1923.

Santa Fe has some prehistory too, right next to the city. I visited when there was a fair amount of snow, which accentuated the beauty of the place. The *La Cienequilla Petroglyph Site* is wonderful, with petroglyphs created between 1100 AD and 1600 AD.[Noble]

You can also visit one of the oldest buildings in America, known as the "*Oldest House*". The earliest foundations beneath the house are the remains of a pueblo and date from 1200 AD. The recognized date of the house is 1646 AD. [De Vargus Street House]

Between 1709 and 1710, the Spanish governor lived there during repairs to the San Miguel Church. In the oldest house, there is a cast of a headless Spanish officer, Juan Espinosa, whose ghost haunts the area.

How to get to Santa Fe historic sites:

Cathedral Basilica of St. Francis of Assisi is located at 131 Cathedral Pl.

San Miguel Mission is located at 401 Old Santa Fe Trail

Loretto Chapel is located at 17 Goodnight Trail E

New Mexico History Museum is located at 113 Lincoln Ave

La Cienequilla Petroglyph Site is located at 662-674 Paseo Real

The Oldest House is located at 215 E De Vargas St #2703

Profiles in history:

St. Francis of Assisi was born in 1181, and was the son of a wealthy merchant in Italy. He wanted to be a noble and a knight, so he became a knight and went on the 4th crusade. He had a dream to return home to an ancient church at San Damiano, where he heard Christ on the crucifix in the church speak to him. *"Francis, repair my church."* He began to preach and people began to follow him. After years of poverty and wandering, he became sick and died of edema on October 4, 1226 at 45 years old. St. Francis was the founder of the Franciscan Order and is the patron saint of Santa Fe, animals, and the environment.

Ghost story:

A Spanish officer, Juan Espinoza, fell in love with a beautiful young woman. He went to the brujas (witches) who lived in the oldest house in Santa Fe. Juan paid the witches many pieces of gold and received a love potion. The potion didn't bring the desired result, and the lady married another man. Juan brandished a sword and demanded the witches give him back the gold.

One of the witches tripped him, he fell and lost his sword. The witch picked up the sword and cut his head off with it. The ghost of Juan Espinoza is said to wander Vargas Street in April when he was murdered, looking for his head.

A moment in time:

In 1680, the ***Pueblo Indian Revolt*** began. It was a well-planned and well-executed rebellion against the harsh rule of Spain. Since the colonization in 1598, the once peaceful Pueblo Indians were treated with severe punishments including whipping, slavery, and hard labor, dismemberment of their hands or feet, and hanging. The Pueblo Indians were forced to destroy objects sacred to them and fill in their ceremonial centers, the kivas, all in an effort to stamp out their religion in favor of Christianity.

Finally after so many decades, they rose up against their Spanish captors, led by a medicine man, named Pope, from the San Juan Pueblo. He led the revolt against the Spanish, on August 10, 1680. Eleven days later, the Spaniards retreated, after the deaths of 400 people, including 21 priests. The Pueblos remained free for twelve years, until 1692, when New Mexico again came under Spanish rule with Governor Pedro de Vargas.

A word about the Dominguez Escalante Expedition:

Two Franciscan priests named Francisco Atanasio Dominguez, who was 36 years old, and 26 year-old Silvestre Velez de Escalante, planned to leave Santa Fe on July 4, 1776, the same day as the signing of the Declaration of Independence.

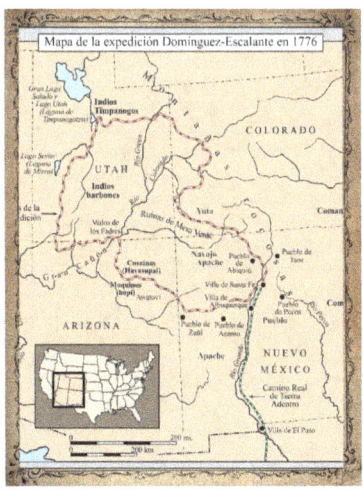

Their goal was to find a route over land from Santa Fe, New Mexico to their mission in Monterey, California. They eventually left Santa Fe on July 29th, traveling over two thousand miles over New Mexico, Colorado, Arizona, and Utah. They never reached Monterey or the Pacific Coast. Crutchfield

Pecos National
Historical Park

*P**ecos National Historical Park*** contains a pueblo which housed 2000 people at its peak. Pecos was founded around 1300 AD and grew to contain 700 rooms. Spanish conquistador Coronado visited Pecos in the 1500's and the Pecos Indians told him to go east because he was looking for gold. They hoped he would get lost.

The Spanish returned in 1590 and by 1610 they had destroyed kivas trying to eradicate the pueblo culture. The original church was destroyed during the pueblo revolt of 1680, and the current church that is standing today was built in 1717. The last people left Pecos in 1838. Noble, NPS

There is a wonderful museum at Pecos National Monument exhibiting beautiful pottery, shell jewelry, an old coffee grinder, assorted items left by the Spanish, and crosses and medals.

How to get to Pecos National Historical Park:

Pecos National Historical Park is located off Hwy 63, near Pecos, New Mexico.

Voices from the past:

"... you will come to the pueblo of Pecos, which has over two thousand souls. Here there is an elegant rectory and temple, of particularly fine and distinct architecture and construction, into which a priest put extraordinary work and care." **Fray Alonso de Benavides, 1630**

A word about kivas:

The word "kiva" means cellar or underground house, and it was a special place of ceremony. Kivas were used primarily by men, but women and children could enter them for certain ceremonies and at certain times. When an area was abandoned, kivas were often ritually closed by being filled in, sealed, and roofs were burned.

Fort Union

F*ort Union* is the site of three different forts built between 1851-1891 to guard the New Mexico territory and protect travelers on the Santa Fe Trail from Apache Indian attacks. Fort Union became the largest fort west of the Mississippi River.

Fort Union was the supply hub for the Southwest, supplying from 30 to 100 wagon trains of up to 200 wagons each daily. 46 regional posts were supplied by Fort Union. NPS

In 1861, a new star-shaped fort was built with 28 cannon platforms to repel the advancing Confederate armies during the Civil War. The confederates were defeated in 1862 at the Battle of Glorieta Pass close to Santa Fe. The confederates left New Mexico, never to return.

A third fort was built to better house the military and supply posts around the Southwest. In 1879, the Atchison, Topeka, and Santa Fe railway began to supply the military, ending the need for Fort Union. The fort closed completely in 1891.

My favorite building is the **Fort Union Jail**. I found it interesting that the jail was located next to the barracks for the enlisted men and their families.

It made me wonder how well the family members slept at night.

There is a *museum* onsite containing many military artifacts including a pair of boots, a meat can, a howitzer and 4-second fuse, and a Civil War bayonet. When you walk the beautiful grounds, you will also see many wagons and large weapons.

How to get to Fort Union:

Fort Union is located just north of the town of Watrous, New Mexico.

Voices from the past:

"Workmen were busy tearing down the old fortification. They tore my heart out with it. Why not let the old walls stand? Around each crumbling wall, each yawning cellar hole, are gathered precious memories of young America" **Marian Sloan Russell, former resident.**

A word about Buffalo Soldiers:

The buffalo soldiers were African American men who were recruited out of the ranks of former slaves to fight in the Civil War. Enlisting in the army enabled them to be promoted and earn a pension. To be in the cavalry, they had to be no taller than 5'9" or 5'10" and weigh no more than 155-160 pounds. They were paid $13 per month, the same as Whites, but they were segregated and many officers refused to lead them. Among those who refused was General Armstrong Custer.

There are three explanations for the name "Buffalo Soldiers" because their curly hair looked like buffalo fur, or they were fierce in battle like a buffalo, or they wore thick coats of buffalo hide in the winter. The Buffalo Soldiers served at Fort Union from 1876-1881 and received all 9 medals of honor given at Fort Union. NPS

Central New Mexico

Salinas Pueblo Missions

Salinas Pueblo Missions

There are three ***Salinas Pueblo Missions***, Abo, Quarai, and Gran Quivira. The Indians who lived at the pueblos were a combination of Ancestral Puebloan (Anasazi) and Mogollon. They began building large communities by 1200 AD. The population in Salinas Valley likely reached at least 10,000 people by the 1600's. They traded salt, corn, beans, squash, and cotton, for buffalo meat and hides, flints, and shells.

The ***Mission of San Gregorio de Abo*** was a large community when the Spaniards came in 1581. The Spanish began converting the Indians of the pueblo in 1622.

The mission church was completed in the late 1620's. The people abandoned the mission between 1672 and 1678. During excavations a large chunk of salt, ready to be traded, was found in a storage room.

Quarai was a large community when Onate came in 1598 to accept it for Spain. Three members of the Spanish Inquisition of the 1600's were at Quarai and presided over cases, including witchcraft, gossip, heresy, blasphemy, use of love potions, and disrespecting the church.

There were several fascinating cases including one that involved the Alcalde Mayor. He allowed the Indians to practice Kachina dances, which caused such disruption at the mission that he was banished by the inquisition.

Another case involved a man named Bernard Gruber, who was accused of superstition. He was put in jail for over 2 years and lost everything, including his health. He escaped but died of thirst in the desert. The desert is called Jornada del Muerto, journey of the dead man.

The church at Quarai is known as Nuestra Senora de la Purisima Concepcion de Cuarac. In 1601, the Indians of the mission rebelled against the Spanish. 900 Indians were killed and 200 were captured.

Quarai Mission has an excellent *museum* containing a number of artifacts, including salt, which was a highly-prized item for trade, and a piece of plaster which once decorated the inside of the church.

Gran Quivira, also called Las Humanas, is the largest of the Salinas Mission ruins. The first church was built in the 1620s. A larger church and mission complex were added 20 years later. Traditionally, women built the church, while the men tended to hunting and weaving.

In the 1660's, friars burned and filled in the existing kivas to get rid of the old religion. The people were weakened from paying tribute to Spain, and from small-pox and flu epidemics.

They also suffered from attacks by plains Indians in the 1600's. In 1668, 450 people died at Gran Quivira from famine. The difficulties they faced lead to the abandonment of Quivira between 1672 and 1675. Noble, NPS

Gran Quivira also has an onsite *museum* containing a ceremonial stone, a ceremonial kiva vessel, and a mountain lion effigy figure

How to get to the Salinas Pueblo Missions:

The Salinas Pueblo Missions are located in three separate areas, close to the town of Mountainair, along Hwy. 60.

A word about the Spanish Inquisition:

The Spanish Inquisition began in 1478 and lasted until 1834, during which time, many thousands died in Spain and in Spanish territories like New Mexico. The Inquisition was charged with exposing people who committed heresy against the Catholic Church. People were brought before the tribunal and coerced into giving up their neighbors.

Punishments dealt out by the Inquisitors were severe and included imprisonment, starvation, confiscation of property, and amputation of limbs. Records indicate the first Inquisitor in Spain, Tomas de Torquemada, burned over 2000 people at the stake.

A moment in time:

The **Battle at Glorieta Pass** has been called the Gettysburg of the West. It occurred in the spring of 1862, more than a year before the battle of Gettysburg. The confederate army attempted to press into the southwest.

Their goal was to take control of mining in Colorado and capture the ports of San Diego and Los Angeles. The battle was fought over 3 days from March 26th through March 28th. Wounded union soldiers were transported to Fort Union, confederates to Santa Fe. Glorieta Pass is located near the Salinas Pueblo Missions. Western National Parks Association

Southwestern New Mexico

Chloride

Gila Cliff Dwellings

The *Gila Cliff Dwellings* are wonderful, but the road to get there will test your driving skills. I took a very windy road that had a number of switchbacks, and it was snowing. It's a 40 mile drive that took me at least 2 hours, but I was rewarded mightily when I finally got there.

The path leading to the spectacular ruins is somewhat steep, but it is paved. The cliff dwellings were built by Mogollon people and date from 1280 AD, although there has been some wood associated with the site that dates back to 1240 AD. ^{Noble, NPS}

It is estimated that 40 to 80 people lived here. You can still see handprints of the builders on one of the walls. It is believed the dwellings were abandoned due to drought. There are some wonderful pictographs at the site, which are still vibrant today.

There is a great little campground at the site called the Lower Scorpion Campground. There are two short paths leading out of the campground. One path leads to some beautiful pictographs, and the other leads to a small two-room cliff dwelling. It's a lovely spot.

There is a ***Visitors Center*** at the Gila Cliff Dwellings, containing artifacts found at or near the site. My favorite is the frog pendant.

As you walk around Gila, be on the lookout for wild pigs, called javelinas, wandering about. They only add to the ambience of the place.

How to get to Gila Cliff Dwellings:

The Gila Cliff Dwellings are located near the town of Silver City. From Silver City, take Hwy 15 North and travel 42 miles to reach the Gila Visitor Center.

Deming

D eming has a wonderful museum known as the ***Luna-Mim-bres Museum***. It's housed in a massive 100-year old build-ing and contains something for everyone including an old ornate clock that was as tall as me, and a war club that was carried by Spotted Eagle, a Lakota Sioux warrior, during the Battle of Little Bighorn.

There are also antique vehicles and an enormous collection of war memorabilia including some Nazi items, Japanese artifacts, canned food rations, and "practice bombs"

There is an area of the museum dedicated to recreating old offices around the town and the equipment they contained. My favorite is the dental office with equipment dating from 1907 to 1946.

As if this isn't enough, one of the star attractions of the museum is the expansive collection of spectacular Mimbres pottery. It is one of the best collections in the Southwest. Luna-Mimbres Museum

How to get to Deming:

Deming is located 60 miles west of Las Cruces, New Mexico off Interstate 10.

Chloride

*C**hloride** began its life in 1879, when Harry Pye, an English-
man, spent the night in a canyon. He took away some rocks
which contained a high concentration of silver chloride. He and

two companions went back to the canyon to get more of the ore. They were attacked by Apaches and Pye was killed.

The two companions got away and word got out about the silver. The town was settled in 1880 at a cost of $1.25 an acre. In June of 1881, Chloride had 3 stores, 3 cafes, 8 saloons, and 2 butcher shops. It did not have a church or a jail.

If someone did something bad, they were dunked in a stock tank and chained to a large oak tree, known as the *"hangin' tree."* Before the decline began, Chloride had about 350 buildings. The town suffered when silver prices went down in 1893.

Today, it's a semi-ghost town with a few friendly people living there. As you walk around Chloride, don't forget to stop in at the *pioneer store*.

It's filled with gazillions of fascinating pieces of history including a dental chair from the 1800's (It's the earliest dental chair I've ever seen) a child's coffin, 1800's clothing, 1800's survey equipment, and millions of old tools.

Remember to visit the *"hangin tree"* in the middle of the street. It's over 200 years old.

How to get to Chloride:

Chloride is located near the city of Truth or Consequences. From T & C, take I-25 north to exit 83. Turn left on Hwy 181, and then left on Hwy 52. Follow signs to Winston, then turn left on Chloride Road.

Lake Valley

*L**ake Valley** was founded in 1878 after silver was found. The silver deposit was named "Bridal Chamber" because of the sparkle of the deposit's crystalline walls. The town was named Lake Valley because of nearby lake beds.

The town started out as a stage stop, but was flooded, so the townsite was moved. It was moved again in 1882 to where it is today.

When you visit Lake Valley to-day, it's hard to believe it once had 12 saloons, 3 churches, 2 newspapers, a school, hotels, and stores.

It also reached a peak popula-tion of 4000 people. Some of the town, including Main Street, was destroyed by fire in 1895. Town of Lake Valley

How to get to Lake Valley:

Lake Valley is located near the town of Nutt. From Nutt, take Hwy 27 north for about 12 miles.

Ghost story:

There is a legend about ***Tommyknockers*** that are said to haunt many mining camps. Tommyknockers got their name from Cornish miners who believed that little men lived underground and caused the knocking with their tiny hammers. Some early miners believed Tommyknockers were good spirits who were warning of an impending mine collapse. Others believed that the person who heard the knocking would die. Still others believed that Tommy-knockers were the spirits of miners who had died during a cave-in. Some miners even left offerings of food and drink to appease the Tommyknockers.

Southern New Mexico

Three Rivers Petroglyph Site

Three Rivers Petroglyph Site

The ***Three Rivers Petroglyph Site*** has over 21,000 petroglyphs laboriously pecked or incised into rock surfaces.

Circles and dots are the most common motifs, representing over 10 percent of the drawings.
Noble, Three Rivers Petroglyph Site

Other images include insects, fish, birds, and animals. The images were made by the Jornada Mogollon between 900 AD and 1400 AD.

It's a beautiful spot, with the snow-capped mountains in the background.

How to get to the Three Rivers Petroglyphs:

The Three Rivers Petroglyph Site is located near the city of Tularosa, at 3 Rivers Rd.

A word about rock art:

There are several cultural periods of rock art, including:

Archaic- 5000 BCE to 300 CE

Basketmaker 1000 BCE to 750 CE (oldest Ancestral Puebloan)

Fremont 500 CE to 1400 CE (Utah and Colorado)

Ancestral Puebloan 200 CE to 1600 CE (N. Arizona and NW New Mexico)

Hohokam 300 CE to 1400 CE (S. Arizona)

Mogollon 500 CE to 1250 CE (SE Arizona and SW New Mexico)

Historic begins 1540 CE after European contact

Smokey the Bear Historical Park

While driving near the Capitan Gap area of New Mexico, I happened upon a place I will never forget. It's where Smokey the Bear is buried. It was a very emotional spot for me because I love animals and had recently lost my dog to cancer.

In 1950, Smokey was found in the Capitan Gap area of New Mexico. He was a small cub just a little over 2 months old, and he was desperately clinging to the limb of a tree. He had been severely burned by a wildfire.

Smokey's burns healed and he was nursed back to health. He grew into an adult and he found a home at the National Zoo in Washington D.C. Smokey became a national symbol of wildfire prevention.

Smokey died in 1976 and is buried at the Smokey the Bear Memorial Park close to the spot where he was found. Smokey Bear Historical Park

How to get to the Smokey Bear Historical Park:

The Smokey Bear Historical Park is located in the town of Capitan, off Hwy. 380.

Lincoln

T he main street in the town of ***Lincoln*** was once known as the "most dangerous street in America." When you walk down the main street today, it's hard to believe it was once the scene of the bloody Lincoln County Wars.

The sleepy, quiet town houses many famous sites from the days of Billy the Kid. There is the **courthouse**, where Billy was incarcerated upstairs, chained to the floor. The courthouse was also the site of the Dolan/Murphy store called "the house."

The bullet holes in the door indicate the spot where Deputy Sheriff J.W. Bell was shot by Billy.

Bell would later stagger outside and die in the yard. Two granite slabs mark the spots where Deputy Sheriff Bell and Deputy Marshall Robert Ollinger died.

Don't miss the **TB Hut.** The hut was built sometime around 1905, by Dr. James Laws, who suffered from tuberculosis himself.

You will also see a unique tower structure, known as the **Torreon.** It was built in the 1850's and was used to protect Spanish Americans from Apache attacks.

Other famous sites include **Dr. Wood's house**, and the **Tunstall Store.** You can also visit the **San Juan Mission Church**, and the **Anderson Freeman Visitors Center.** Balfour

How to get to Lincoln:

Lincoln is located 57 miles west of Roswell, New Mexico.

Voices from the past:

" William bonney was incarcerated first time, December 22, 1878; Second time, March 21, 1879, and I hope I never will be again. W.H. Bonney" **written in the Lincoln Jail by Billy the Kid**

A word about the Lincoln County Wars:

The ***Lincoln County Wars*** began in the spring of 1877. The wars were fought over stealing cattle and horses. The rustling and rebranding went on for about 2 years.

There were two factions, the Chisum, Tunstall, and Mcsween group, and the Dolan, Murphy, Morton, Baker, and Daniels group. Billy was fond of Tunstall and when Tunstall was murdered, Billy became involved in the conflict.

Profiles in history:

William H. Bonney, commonly known as "Billy the Kid" was born in New York, Nov. 23 1859. His father died when Billy was young, so young Billy worshipped his mother, and was gentlemanly toward the ladies. His life of crime began when he was 12, when he punched a man who insulted his mother. He was kept from killing the man by Ed Moulton. Then Billy stabbed a man to death who was trying to kill Ed Moulton. Billy the Kid became an outlaw by defending others. He never saw his beloved mother again.

Billy was described by Pat Garrett, the man who killed him, as a man who "could not stay whipped." If Billy lost a fight, he would seek out guns and use them with "murderous intent." Pat Garrett recounts that Billy killed Indians, Spaniards, and killed as many people as he had years. That would mean Billy killed 21 people, but the exact amount of deaths attributed to Billy is closer to 6. He was jailed in the Lincoln county courthouse, which was previously the Murphy Dolan building, known as *the house*. Billy was guarded by JW Bell deputy sheriff, whom he liked, and deputy marshal Ollinger whom he did not like.

Patrick Garrett
[1850-1908]

During his confinement, Billy talked with Pat Garrett about why he did the things he did. Billy didn't want sympathy, and he respected Pat Garrett and didn't feel any hatred towards him. Billy felt Garrett was just doing his duty. Billy escaped from jail by shooting both Bell and Ollinger. Pat Garrett tracked him to the home of Billy's friend, Lucien Maxwell. Billy was shot and killed. He was buried at Fort Sumner on July 15, 1881. Billy was 21 years, 7 months, and 21 days old, according to Pat Garrett. Billy had never fired a shot. Pat Garrett was unsure whether Billy recognized who he was or not. Enss, Garrett

Roswell

R oswell's claim to fame is the ***International UFO Museum***. I wasn't sure whether to include this in a book about history, but it does have some historical value.

There are numerous newspaper clippings and information about Area 51, and the UFO crash that happened at Roswell back in the day. Along with the historical bits and pieces. Be prepared to be greeted by alien statues and other items a UFO fanatic will love.

How to get to Roswell:

Roswell is located in southeastern New Mexico, off Hwy 380 and Hwy 285.

A moment in time:

It was July, 1947, when the *"Roswell Incident"* happened, forever changing the sleepy town. Metallic fabric and rubber parts were recovered by Army Air Field Personnel. The items belonged to a top-secret military balloon which was part of Project Mogul. The goal of the project was to listen for Soviet atomic testing, using countless balloons which were launched into the air. One of these balloons crashed at Roswell.

Decades and many conspiracy theories later, the "Roswell Incident" has become a piece of folklore, much celebrated by the town of Roswell. You can catch up on all the various theories about government conspiracies, alien autopsies, and more, by visiting the Roswell UFO Museum.

Fun Facts about UFOs:

In 1947, Kenneth Arnold, a pilot, first used the term UFO, or unidentified flying object.

There were 12,618 UFO sightings from 1948-69, of which only 701 are still unidentified.

You can buy insurance to compensate for an alien abduction.

In 1639, John Winthrop, governor of the Massachusetts Bay Colony, documented a strange sighting of lights in the sky.

More UFO sightings have occurred in the Northern U.S. than in Southern U.S.

Carlsbad Caverns

T he ***Carlsbad Caverns*** are an awe-inspiring network of 119 known caves which are 4 to 6 million years old. The many stalactites, stalagmites, draperies, and other rock decorations started 500,000 years ago, during a wetter climate. NPS

I descended down the spiraling "natural entrance" which is a path that descends down what is the length of the Empire State Building.

The further down I descended, the darker it got. Thankfully, the interior had a fair degree of lighting, making the rock features look like eerie, alien life-forms.

The caverns are also home to hundreds of thousands of free-tailed bats, which you can see at a separate entrance.

How to get to Carlsbad Caverns:

Carlsbad Caverns are located near White's City, off Hwy. 7.

Eastern New Mexico

Blackwater Draw

Fort Sumner

*F**ort Sumner*** is named for the fort built here in 1862 to guard the Bosque Redondo Indian Reservation. It is also another important site relating to Billy the Kid. It's the site where Billy the

Kid was shot and killed by Sheriff Pat Garrett on July 14, 1881 in his friend Lucien Maxwell's house. [Garrett]

Billy the Kid's grave is there too. The large tombstone was placed in 1931. Billy resides next to his friends, Tom O'Folliard and Charlie Bowdre. In addition to their names, the headstone reads "PALS"

The **Billy the Kid Museum** is in Fort Sumner, and it's a wonderful place to go visit. The museum is family-run and I had the pleasure of talking with a very knowledgeable member of the family, whose dad was alive during Billy the Kid's lifetime and new all about Billy.

In addition to having a nice collection of antique vehicles, including a hearse, the museum has some fascinating artifacts. My favorites include Billy's rifle and the drapes from the bedroom where Billy was killed.

How to get to Fort Sumner:

Fort Sumner is located about 162 miles southeast of Albuquerque, off Hwy. 60 east.

A word about the Bosque Redondo Indian Reservation:

The Bosque Redondo Indian Reservation was an internment center from 1863 to 1868 for Navajo and Mescalero Apache Indians. Prior to their confinement, over 50 Native American groups were forced to walk from their ancestral homelands to Fort Sumner, a distance of over 300 miles. Many died before reaching the reservation. Others were shot. Even pregnant women would be killed if they couldn't keep up. Once they reached the reservation, the Indians were forbidden to practice their religions.

Food was also rationed, and what food they did receive was often not familiar to them. They also suffered from severe cold and a type of disease like smallpox, which they acquired from military personnel. It is estimated that disease, exposure, and lack of food led to the deaths of 1500 people. Finally, in 1868, a treaty was signed which allowed the survivors to return to their homelands. The Bosque Redondo Memorial was created in 2005 to tell the stories of the Navajo and Apache, who made what the Navajo call "the Long Walk."

Blackwater Draw

***B**lackwater Draw* is one of those sites where the history of man in North America began. At *t*he site, evidence of the Clovis culture from 12,000 years ago was discovered. At that time, the now arid site was a marshy pond surrounded by trees and grasses.

As I walked along the trail that runs the perimeter of the ancient pond, it was hard for me to imagine this rocky, inhospitable place once being the home of woolly mammoths and the ancient hunters who stalked them.

Thousands of years ago, Clovis hunters killed the animals. The animal remains, which included mammoths and camels, along with tools and arrow points, became buried in the mud layers.

These same artifacts were discovered thousands of years later and are now housed in a climate-controlled building at the site.

Excavations are ongoing, and you will see layers of bones and tools from the Clovis Culture of 11,040 to 11,630 years ago and the later Folsom Culture of 10,170 to 10, 490 years ago. Noble, Texas Parks and Wildlife

There is a small **museum**, located offsite in Portales, which houses some of the artifacts from Blackwater Draw including Clovis points, spear points, and a handaxe, which are 12,000 years old. There is also a fragment of mammoth tusk, and an ancient horse tooth.

At Blackwater, gravel mining began after World War II and many bones and artifacts were destroyed. In 1962, five mammoths and an ancient bison were found with Clovis artifacts, which led to the protection of the site. So far, 28 mammoths have been found along with ice-age bison.

The oldest excavated well in North America is also at Blackwater Draw.

How to get to Blackwater Draw:

The Blackwater Draw Site is located near Portales, and the Museum is located in Portales.

Favorite Places to Camp

City of Rocks State Park is the perfect location to explore Deming, Lake Valley, and surrounding areas. The park has 41 developed campsites, BBQ pits, showers, toilets, and water. You can find more information at New Mexico State Parks, or make a reservation online at *reserveamerica.com.*

Sumner Lake State Park is an excellent base camp to explore Fort Sumner, Blackwater Draw, and surrounding areas. The park offers 50 developed campsites, and also primitive campsites. Amenities include showers, toilets, and water. For more information or to make a reservation, contact *reserveamerica.com.*

Three Rivers Petroglyph Campground is a great starting point to visit the petroglyphs on site, Smokey the Bear Historical Park, Lincoln, and surrounding areas. This BLM campground has five shelter sites, one group site, two RV sites with hookups, and five tent sites. To find out more, visit **https://www.blm.gov/visit/three-rivers-petroglyph-site**

Storrie Lake Campground is perfect for exploring Santa Fe and the surrounding area. The campground offers 29 campsites with electricity, water, showers, and toilets, plus wonderful views of the lake. To find out more or to make reservations, visit **reserveamerica.com**

Random Thoughts
What History Means to Me

F irst, let me start by sharing with you my opinion of what history isn't. History is not a collection of random dates, names, and places for you to memorize. History is not a dry and uninteresting class you have to pass to graduate.

I believe history is a tangible thing. You can actually *feel* history in the places you go, and the sights you see. I remember walking up to the Acropolis in Athens. I looked down at the well-worn marble steps and wondered about how many ancient philosophers had climbed these very steps, thousands of years ago.

You don't have to go far away to experience the *feeling* of history. If you are lucky enough to live in an old house, you may experience history in your own surroundings. You might say to yourself, *"If only these walls could talk."*

During my travels across the United States, I *felt* history in many, many places. If you travel across the country like I did, you will *feel* the wonderful history of our beautiful country for yourself, and you will never be the same. You will discover what it means to be an American.

Why I did it and why you can too:

I decided to travel across the country by car because I wanted to rediscover America. When I first set out to explore the history of our country, I wanted to find out why America is the greatest country on earth, and what it means to be an American.

The politics of these United States was frightening at the time. Our country was polarized, almost beyond repair. Whether it was Democrats or Republicans, Conservatives, or Liberals, everyone was fighting.

I wanted to rediscover the joy of being an American. I wanted to rediscover our rich history, our unique and wonderful people, our tapestry of multicultural heritage, and our rich natural resources. I thought a road trip by car across eleven western states was a good place to start.

I have a degree in Archaeology, and a passion for all things archaeological. I love history, with a side love of paleontology. It is these three passions that I set my trip agenda around. I set out to discover the archaeological sites, history, and paleontological world of our country.

As I travel and write my books, I get asked all the time, especially by women, "What is it like to travel by yourself? Aren't you scared?" The truth is, I believe everyone should do what I did. It's a wonderful way to discover our country, and to rediscover yourself. The truth is, I'm scared not to travel. Traveling allows you to get to know yourself, in ways not possible when sitting on the couch watching TV.

We tend to spend a lot of our lives tuning out the world and our place within it. When you travel, you are quite literally forced to deal with your own thoughts, emotions, and feelings. You can discover yourself while traveling. You can come to understand what makes you who you are, and how you can perhaps become a better person. Above all, traveling gives you mental clarity to figure out how to live with intent. It's a way to guide your life, not just wait for things to happen.

Travel Tips & Stuff

What You Need to Know

How to get started:

P lanning your trip should be one of the most exciting things about it. You want to be spontaneous, but it is also very wise to plan your route, so you can take full advantage of all the time and miles you will invest.

- First, decide your passions. If you love airplanes, trains, or old vehicles, plan your trip around that. If you love gardens or architecture, seek that out as the focus of your trip.

- Next, read and research areas of the country that will let you enjoy what you are interested in.

- Make a list by state and city or town, of what you want to see.

- Take your handy road atlas and locate the areas on the pages.

- Make a tentative route plan, so you have an idea of where you are going.

Travel tip: Avoid trying to plan your trip down to a schedule of days, hours, or minutes. On a road trip, it will be virtually impossible to know where you will be on any given day. If you adhere to a schedule, you are more likely to stress out, and less likely to actually enjoy yourself, which is the whole point.

What you need:

You need to bring along a sense of adventure and a curious mind. You need to ditch the idea of always being on a schedule, and live a little more spontaneously to thoroughly enjoy yourself. Things will happen as you travel, both good things and bad things, and you need to prepare your mind and your soul for day-to-day changes.

So much of our lives are planned out. Between growing up, going to school, finding a career, marriage, kids, or whatever, people have lost much of the ability to be spontaneous. But you must take spontaneity on the trip with you, because you may make detours along the way to see something really spectacular.

So, for the practical stuff you need:

A great vehicle-I have a Honda CRV which is fabulous. It's old, a 2004, fully paid for, and will go anywhere. I see humongous RVs on the road, towing a car behind, and all I can think of is, they can't go just anywhere. They are too big. Bad gas mileage, cumbersome to drive, slow, and not agile like my CRV. So, I encourage you, if you want to go car camping and be able to go on remote dirt roads, get an agile vehicle, and Hondas are great.

Travel tip: Don't be afraid to do some modifications to your vehicle. I took one of my back seats out. (after watching a YouTube video) I threw in a twin mattress, a bit of drapery, and some netting. I also put some of those little portable light switches on the inside. I jettisoned anything I hadn't used up to that point. Don't be afraid to get rid of unnecessary stuff.

An awesome camera that you know inside and out. I use a Nikon and it takes wonderful pictures. Don't skimp on a camera, and don't think a cellphone camera is all you need, because you want the best for your beautiful photos.

A hot plate warmer-this little item was indispensable. You need a converter for it so you can plug it in to the cigarette lighter. Place your food inside it, carton and all, and then plug it in. 30 minutes for thawed food, about an hour and a half for frozen food. Boom! You have a hot meal by the time you stop for the night!

Window shades-the best ones are magnetic so you just place them against your windows and they cling to them, obscuring the view inside your car.

Portable cooler with wheels-another indispensable item that works great and is easy to move around. I use those nifty blue frozen blocks in mine.

Portable air compressor-this little gem plugs into your cigarette lighter and will inflate your tires if you have a flat. Fortunately, I haven't had to use this yet.

Portable battery charger and power bank-mine comes with battery cables and the power bank, yet once inside the case, it is small enough to put in your glove compartment. This little item, unfortunately, I have had to use, and it saved me.

Portable generator-mine came with a small solar panel, so it can be charged with solar or electricity. It has a decent battery life and also doubles as a light for night-time.

All season clothing-you never know what different states will bring for weather, so take hot weather and cold weather clothes, and a fair amount of shoes appropriate for hiking, or walking, sandals, and slippers, which are nice at night. Also take along a pair of cheap rubber flip-flops to wear in the public showers you might go into.

Your own pillows-I like my own pillows, so I don't wake up with neck cramps, especially after sleeping in the car.

Sleeping bag and cozy blankets-you want to stay warm and layering is everything.

Warm hat, warm socks, and fuzzy jammies to keep you warm for cold nights sleeping in the car.

A great road atlas, and great guidebooks-get one that's easy to read, with great pictures. For a road atlas, just get one that is easy to read.

A word about photography:

Along with a great camera, you need to have a great eye. This is easier than it sounds once you have worked with your camera and are comfortable taking pictures with it. I am not a professional photographer, but I like my pictures and other people do too.

These are my tips for taking great pictures:

- Experiment with taking both horizontal and vertical shots.

- Don't always put the subject of the photo in the middle of the photograph.

- This one is important: pay attention to the foreground,

and if possible, have something, a plant or whatever, in the foreground to help give the photo dimension and depth.

- This one is important too: turn around often to see the view you just came from. I do this quite often and some of my best pictures have resulted from when I turned around and took the shot.

You can also take a mental photo. Place an image in your mind that you can call upon later. Use all of your senses to see, hear, smell, and maybe even to taste, what is around you. You have the means to fully experience your surroundings, and that is very important to a traveler. When you take a mental photo, be sure to jot down quick little details about what you saw, heard, smelled, or tasted, so you can jog your memory later.

And last, but not least...don't be posing in front of everything, everywhere, to show that you actually went somewhere. Most people want to see themselves in your photo and be mentally transported there, but they can't if you are there already.

To camp or not to camp:

Car camping is great. I prefer it to sleeping on the cold, hard ground in a tent. I can lock the doors, put my window shades up and be cozy for the night.

That being said, for me there were some do's and don'ts about camp sites. Some people camp in a Walmart parking lot and feel safe. I do not. I believe that if you are in a busy area, you're more likely to be confronted by a nut job who may bother you. Nothing against Walmart.

Same goes for casino parking lots. Many people believe that if they are in a public place, there is less chance of someone bothering them. I don't share this belief. I believe you are safer parked out in the middle of nowhere in the dark. That same nut job who can find you in a parking lot is not about to go driving around on dirt roads to see if anyone is parked there. At least that's my belief. You may not share it, and that's fine. Park and camp wherever you feel safe.

I don't go for rest areas either because they have a track record of incidents happening to people in rest areas, especially women travelers.

So, where do I camp? In state or national campgrounds, wildlife sanctuaries, or off on a dirt road somewhere, usually out in the middle of nowhere.

There are definitely times when I stay in a motel. I use Hotels.com because I like their stay 10 nights, get 1 night free deal. So, I book a hotel or motel if:

- The weather is too hot or too cold, or too rainy

- I am in a city and plan to stay awhile

- I'm tired of camping, need a shower, or my body hurts

- I need to do laundry

A word about safety:

When you are a woman traveling alone, it's critical to keep a low profile. Don't tell people you are traveling alone, where you are staying, or any other personal information.

I don't go to bars or get drunk. I'm not preaching but you are on your own, in a city or town you've never been to, and you don't know anyone, so it's not the time to lose control of what you are doing. When you are in control, you are better able to decide which people you want to get to know better.

Travel tip: If you feel vulnerable traveling alone, that's OK. Vulnerability is part of passion, and traveling is a passionate thing to do. You can put one of those family stickers on your vehicle to indicate to others that you are not traveling alone, which can help you feel more secure.

Maintain your connections:

When you are traveling alone, there is a definite sense of disconnection. It feels almost like you are the only one in the world, traveling through space and time. That's why it's critical to keep your connections to loved ones active.

Be on Facebook while you are traveling. You may not have internet a lot of the time, or the internet will be poor. Consider paying to have your phone be a hotspot. It's a little bit of money per month, but it's worth it and has saved me from being without internet. I love the convenience of it, and you will too.

Plan your journey around visiting family members or friends you haven't seen for a long time, or people that are good friends. When you see people you know, it will ground you, so you can continue traveling.

Check in by phone with loved ones. They worry about you, and it's good for both of you to stay connected no matter where you are.

Consider traveling with a pet. I started my trip with my beloved 14-year-old sheltie named Sadie. She didn't make it to the end of the trip. I lost her to bladder cancer about four months in. My Sadie was special, and I will never forget my first traveling buddy.

It took me a solid year to decide on getting another dog. I poured over profiles of rescue dogs, looking for a little buddy I could take care of. Best Friends Animal Society in Kanab, Utah, had my perfect match. I now have Rosie, an 8 year-old sheltie that looks just like Sadie and has many of the same mannerisms. Life is good again.

I highly recommend Best Friends Animal Society if you are looking for a pet. They have 3000 acres and house up to 1600 animals at one time including dogs, cats, horses, pigs, and just about everything else. The dedicated people at Best Friends are wonderful both to you, and your potential pet.

Travel tip: One of the easiest and best ways I stay connected while traveling is to offer to take a photo for someone I don't know. Many couples, families, or singles would love to have more pictures of themselves traveling. It's an easy and quick way to have a connection with a fellow traveler, and it's good manners too.

—◦❖◦—

Practical matters:

You need to have an address to send your mail to. Keep in touch with whomever is nice enough to do this for you.

You will also need to come back occasionally to register your car, vote, go to doctor visits, and take care of any other business. You can't leave it all behind, as tempting as that may be.

Bad things that happened:

Remember when I said you need to take spontaneity with you on your trip? Well, there were many times when I used my spontaneity skillset.

The government shutdown happened smack dab in the middle of my travels. That meant that all of the National Monuments were closed. I did a lot of driving and circling around.

I also did a lot of circling around trying to avoid natural disasters. I traveled through Paradise, California shortly before a massive fire happened there. I tried to travel through the area again but was pushed out by massive flooding. My latest event was camping in Canyonville, Oregon and waking up to flames creeping down the hillside. That was day one of the Canyonville fire.

Besides being driven out by natural disasters, sometimes I was driven out by rude people. Many times it was centered around my furry traveling companion. I believe there are really only two types of people, those who love animals and those who don't.

When people see me walking my beautiful, sweet, elderly dog, they either come up and pet her, or they say something harsh.

One incident was a woman, a total stranger, who came up to me smiling down at Sadie and asked how old she was. I replied, "She is 13 and a half years old." The woman replied very curtly "She needs to be put down." Sadie was walking around, alert, and happy, and yet this woman wanted me to end her life because she was old.

Speaking of animals, several times I came very close to driving into an animal on the road. I can't stress enough how many times this will happen to you, and all I can say is, be alert at all times while you are driving. When you travel a lot of miles, you will get tired, so stop and smell the roses, and try not to drive at night.

Good things that happened:

One of the sheer joys of taking a road trip is the unpredictability of it. You never know what you will see. I am originally from Oregon, and bears are not a common sight. So, while driving high up in the Blue Mountains, I looked over and saw a bear! So exciting! He didn't stay for long, kind of shy, but so cute. I love animals, so to see the rich and wonderful amount of wildlife in our country gladdened my heart.

I met many great people on my trip, from all walks of life. They were a walking, talking advertisement for our beautiful country. I smiled at them, and they smiled back. We are all Americans, and we are all part of the human race. When you meet people across the country, you realize just how important it is to get to know your fellow citizens, and learn more about how they view the world and our country.

I have to give a special shout-out to the many dedicated people, often volunteers, who staff our state and national parks and monuments. They work tirelessly to ensure the health of our natural resources, and help travelers enjoy their visit. The same is true of the many people who staff the museums in small towns and large cities. They enjoy history, like I do, and it shows in their smiles.

Along with wonderful people, I have seen an America that is spectacularly beautiful, with open prairies, majestic mountains, and crystal clear rivers. I have seen a small fraction of the history of our country. I have seen the memorials to the brave people who shaped our country. I have fallen in love with America in a way that was not possible sitting in my living room. People ask me, "would I do it again?" The answer comes easily, "Yes, in a heartbeat."

Bibliography and Further Reading

Balfour, Amy C. Southwest USA's Best Trips: 32 Amazing Road Trips. Lonely Planet, 2014.

Bandelier National Monument Main Loop Trail Guide, Western National Parks Association

Benavides, Alonso de., and Baker H. Morrow. A Harvest of Reluctant Souls: Fray Alonso De Benavides's History of New Mexico, 1630. University of New Mexico Press, 2012.

Billy the Kid's Old Fort Sumner, Billy the Kid Museum

Blackwater Draw, Texas Parks and Wildlife

Carlsbad Caverns National Park, National Park Service

Chaco Culture, National Park Service

Chino, Conroy. Petroglyphs of the Southwest: a Puebloan Perspective. Western National Parks Association, 2012.

Civil War Battle of Glorieta Pass Trail Guide, Western National Parks Association, 2009.

Coronado Historic Site, New Mexico Department of Cultural Affairs, 2015.

Diamond, Jared M. Collapse: How Societies Choose to Fail or Succeed. Penguin Books, 2011.

Edmund, Donald. The Stories They Told Us, Life in the Old West. Not Listed, 2017.

El Morro, National Park Service

Enss, Chris. Object, Matrimony: the Risky Business of Mail-Order Matchmaking on the Western Frontier. Globe Pequot Press, 2013.

Enss, Chris. Tales behind the Tombstones. Morris Pub., 2007.

Enss, Chris. The Doctor Wore Petticoats: Women Physicians of the Old West. TwoDot, 2006.

Experience New Mexico's National Parks, National Park Service

Finch, etc. al.., Jackie. Eyewitness Travel USA. DK Publishing, 2017.

Fort Union A Photo History, Southwest Parks and Monuments Association, 1991.

Fort Union Buffalo Soldiers: The 9th U.S. Cavalry, National Park Service

Fort Union, National Park Service

Garrett, Pat F. The Authentic Life of Billy the Kid. University of Oklahoma Press, 1954.

Gila Cliff Dwellings, National Park Service

Glassman, Steve. It Happened on the Santa Fe Trail. Twodot, 2008.

Guide to the Inscription Trail, Western National Parks Association, 2008.

Hill, William E. The Oregon Trail, Yesterday and Today: a Brief History and Pictorial Journey along the Wagon Tracks of Pioneers. Caxton Press, 2014.

Historic Chloride, Geronimo Trail National Scenic Byway

Jemez Historic Site, New Mexico Department of Cultural Affairs, 2015.

Krause, Mariella. Southwest USA's Best Trips: 32 Amazing Trips. Lonely Planet, 2014.

Mayo, Matthew P. Haunted Old West: Phantom Cowboys, Spirit-Filled Saloons, Mystical Mine Camps, and Spectral Indians. Globe Pequot Press, 2012.

Noble, David Grant. Ancient Ruins and Rock Art of the Southwest: an Archaeological Guide. Taylor Trade Publishing, 2015.

Noble, David Grant. Ancient Ruins of the Southwest: an Archaeological Guide. Northland Pub., 2000.

Old Spanish Trail, Bureau of Land Management, 2012.

The Oldest House, De Vargus Street House

Pecos, National Park Service

Reliquary, The Cathedral Basilica of St. Francis of Assisi

Rutter, Michael. Bedside Book of Bad Girls: Outlaw Women of the American West. Farcountry Press, 2008.

Salinas Pueblo Missions, National Park Service

Scott, Robert. Plain Enemies: Best True Stories of the Frontier West. Caxton Printers, 1995.

Shakespeare Ghost Town, Friends of Shakespeare

Simmons, Marc. Yesterday in Sante Fe Episodes in a Turbulent History. Sunstone Press, 1989.

Slater, John M., and Lawrence Clark Powell. El Morro, Inscription Rock, New Mexico: the Rock Itself, the Inscriptions Thereon, and the Travelers Who Made Them. Plantin Press, 1961.

Three Rivers Petroglyphs, Three Rivers Petroglyphs

Wagner, Tricia Martineau. It Happened on the Oregon Trail: Remarkable Events That Shaped History. GPP, 2014.

Index

Referenced by Sections

National Historic Park, Fort Union, Salinas Pueblo Missions, Three Rivers Petroglyph Site, Lincoln, Fort Sumner

B

Baley, America-see El Morro

Bandelier, Adolph-see Bandelier National Monument

Barba, Diego Martin-see El Morro

Basketmaker culture-see Three Rivers Petroglyph Site

Battle at Glorieta Pass-see Fort Union, Salinas Pueblo Missions

Battle of Kennon's Landing-see El Morro

Bell, Sheriff J.W. -see Lincoln

Bern, Switzerland-see Bandelier National Monument

Billy the Kid-see Lincoln, Fort Sumner

Billy the Kid Museum-see Fort Sumner

Billy the Kid's Grave-see Fort Sumner

Bonney, Willam H-see Lincoln, Fort Sumner

Bosque Redondo Indian Reservation-see Fort Sumner

Breckenridge, Peachy-see El Morro

Bridal Camber-see Lake Valley

brujas-see Santa Fe

buffalo soldiers-see Fort Union

About the Author

Julie Bettendorf is a world traveler with a degree in archaeology and a background in history. She has traveled extensively throughout Egypt, Central America, South America, Europe, and the United Kingdom, visiting archaeological and historical sites all along the way.

Currently, Julie is traveling around the US visiting ghost towns, ancient rock art sites, and archaeological wonders as part of research for her ongoing historical travel series entitled *Wandering*

Woman. Wandering Woman is a set of state-by-state guides, full of photographs, historical anecdotes, and unique tips to help other women travel and explore solo across the US by car. Julie enjoys writing freelance blogs, traveling frequently with her two adult children, and hiking outdoors with her faithful dog companion Rosie.

Also By Julie Bettendorf

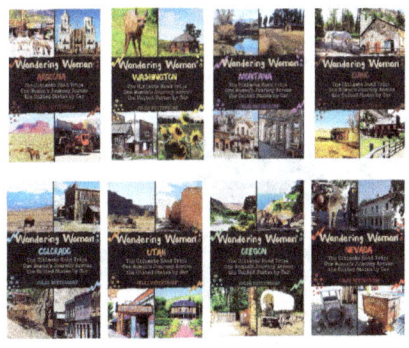

Wandering Woman: New Mexico is the ninth book in the ***Wandering Woman Travel Series***. The first eight books ***Wandering Woman: Montana***, ***Wandering Woman: Utah, Wandering Woman: Nevada, Wandering Woman: Colorado, Wandering Woman: Idaho, Wandering Woman: Washington, Wandering Woman: Oregon, and Wandering Woman: Arizona*** are available in ebook and paperback.

 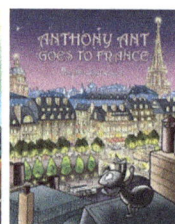

Julie has published two children's books in an ongoing, beautifully illustrated travel series entitled ***Anthony Ant Goes to France*** and ***Anthony Ant Goes to Egypt***.

She has also published a work of historical fiction entitled ***Luxor: Book of Past Lives*** which has recently been released as an audiobook, read by renowned narrator Barry Shannon.